GW01239906

Session Skills
for Bass
Grades 3-5

Published by
Trinity College London
trinitycollege.com
Registered in England
Company no. 09726123

Copyright © 2015 Trinity College London
Second impression, April 2017

Printed in England by Caligraving Ltd.
Written, recorded and produced by Camden Music Services.
Exercises devised by Sam Burgess, backing tracks by Tom Fleming.

SESSION SKILLS

CONTENTS

 CD1 tuning track

 CD2 tuning track

SESSION SKILLS

INTRODUCTION

To be a great rock and pop musician you need to develop a range of important musical skills – from performing with flair to improvising and picking up new songs quickly. Trinity College London's Rock & Pop exams are designed to help you develop these skills and take your musicianship to the next level.

An important part of each Rock & Pop exam is the **session skills** test. For this you can choose either **playback** or **improvising**:

- **Playback** involves playing some music you have not seen or heard before, testing your ability to pick up new musical material quickly

- **Improvising** involves performing an improvisation over a backing track, testing your ability to respond creatively to a specified musical style and chord sequence.

About this book

This book is specially designed to help you prepare for the session skills test at Grades 3 to 5, whether you choose playback or improvising. It contains plenty of example tests to use for practice, as well as two CDs of backing tracks. It also includes specific guidance on how to approach playback and improvising at Grades 3, 4 and 5.

Please note that Rock & Pop exams require you to perform three songs as well as the session skills test. A range of songs for each grade level are provided in a separate series of Rock & Pop song books, also published by Trinity. Additional songs can be downloaded at www.trinityrock.com, where you can also find the syllabus and a range of resources for teaching and learning. The syllabus can change from time to time, so check the website regularly to make sure you are referring to an up-to-date version.

SESSION SKILLS

THE TESTS

Playback

If you choose playback for the session skills test, you'll be asked to perform some music you have not seen or heard before. You'll be given a song chart and 30 seconds to study it and try out any sections. The examiner will then play the backing track.

You should listen to the backing track, playing back what you hear and reading the music from the song chart if you want. You'll hear a series of short melodic phrases - you should repeat each of these straight back in turn. A count-in will be given at the beginning of the backing track, and a backing rhythm will play throughout.

In the exam you'll have two chances to play along with the backing track: first time for practice and second time for assessment. If you choose to read the music from the song chart, remember that for each repeated phrase you should listen the first time and play the second time.

Improvising

If you choose improvising for the session skills test, you'll be asked to improvise in a specific style over a backing track you have not heard before. You'll be given a chord chart, and the examiner will play a short section of the backing track to give you a feel for the tempo and style. You'll have 30 seconds to study the chord chart and try out any sections. The examiner will then play the backing track.

You should improvise in the specified style over the backing track, which will consist of four repetitions of the chord sequence shown on the chord chart. A count-in will be given at the beginning of the backing track, and a backing rhythm will play throughout.

In the exam you'll have two chances to play along with the backing track: first time for practice and second time for assessment. A count-in will be given both times.

SESSION SKILLS

PARAMETERS

Trinity provides a full set of parameters for the session skills tests. Published online at www.trinityrock.com, these tell you which musical elements are featured in improvising and playback at each grade. All the example tests in this book have been written to fit with these parameters, so you can be sure that the test in the exam will be similar to the examples in this book.

The following is a summary of the parameters for Grades 3 to 5. Visit www.trinityrock.com for the full set of parameters across all grades.

Playback

For bass players at Grades 3 and 4, playback is 8 to 12 bars long. At Grade 5 it is 12 to 16 bars long. Within this, each phrase is either two or four bars long. At Grade 3 the time signature can be $\frac{4}{4}$, $\frac{2}{4}$ or $\frac{3}{4}$, with $\frac{6}{8}$ appearing at Grade 4 and $\frac{12}{8}$ at Grade 5.

A wide range of note values are used at Grades 3 to 5. At Grade 3 you can expect to see minims (half notes), crotchets (quarter notes), semibreves (whole notes), swung and straight quavers (eighth notes) and semiquavers (sixteenth notes). Dotted minims, dotted crotchets and ties can also appear, as well as crotchet, minim, semibreve and quaver rests. Grade 4 features the same range of note values with the addition of quaver triplets, dotted crotchet rests and syncopation. At Grade 5, dotted quavers and dotted minim rests are added.

Various dynamics and articulations are featured in playback at Grades 3 to 5. Grades 3 and 4 can contain *p*, *f*, *mp*, *mf*, staccato, legato, accents, crescendo and diminuendo, with *pp*, *ff* and *sfz* featured at Grade 5.

Two new keys are added at each grade level between Grade 3 and Grade 5. In addition to the keys already introduced at Grade 2 (A minor, E minor, C major, G major, F major and D minor), D major and B minor are added at Grade 3. A major and C minor are added at Grade 4, and E major and G minor are added at Grade 5. At all three grades the blues scale can also be used. Chord symbols appear on the song chart at Grade 5, and chromatic melody notes can also appear at this level.

Second position is introduced at Grade 3, as well as hammer-ons and pull-offs. Slides and double-stopping can appear at Grade 4, and up to fifth position can be used at Grade 5.

SESSION SKILLS

PARAMETERS

Improvising

For bass players at Grade 3, the chord sequence is eight bars long with one chord per bar. At Grade 4 it is also eight bars long though with some use of two chords per bar. At Grade 5 the sequence is 12 bars long, also with some use of two chords per bar. The backing track always consists of four repetitions of the chord sequence. The time signature can be $\frac{3}{4}$ or $\frac{4}{4}$ at Grade 3, with the addition of $\frac{6}{8}$ at Grade 4 and $\frac{12}{8}$ at Grade 5. Swung quavers (eighth notes) can feature at all three grades.

In addition to keys featured at earlier grades, at Grade 3 the chord sequence can be in B minor or G minor. E major and C minor can also appear at Grade 4, and B major and F minor at Grade 5. Dominant 7th chords can appear at Grade 3, major and minor 7th chords at Grade 4, and sus4 chords at Grade 5.

Improvising at Grades 3 to 5 can be in a range of styles. In addition to simple rock, pop, ballad, heavy rock and country, which can all appear at Grade 2, Grade 3 can also feature blues style. At Grade 4 reggae and R'n'B can appear, and Grade 5 can include funk, shuffle and disco.

GRADE 3 PLAYBACK

Example 1

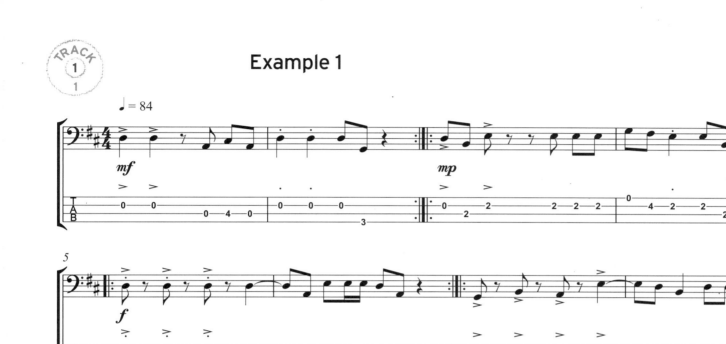

⚡ **TOP TIP** Notice the semiquavers which appear in playback from Grade 3 onwards. Listen carefully to these in the backing track and try to capture them clearly in your performance.

Example 2

Example 3

Example 4

Example 5

Example 6

Example 7

Example 8

Example 9

Example 10

GRADE 3 IMPROVISING

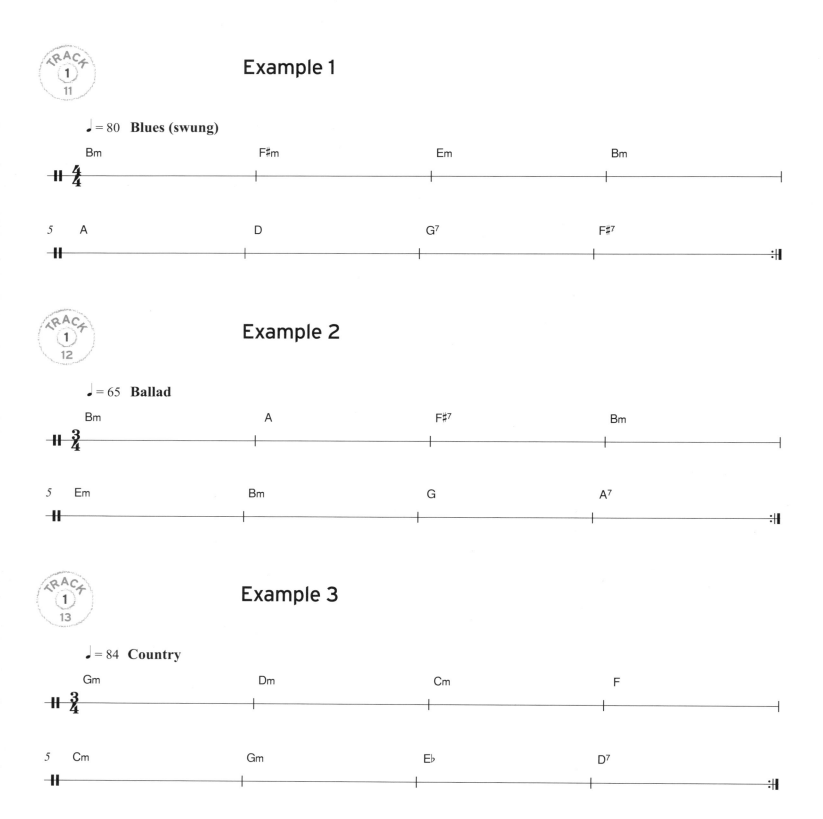

Example 1

TRACK 1 / 11

♩ = 80 **Blues (swung)**

Bm	F♯m	Em	Bm

5 A	D	G⁷	F♯⁷

Example 2

TRACK 1 / 12

♩ = 65 **Ballad**

Bm	A	F♯⁷	Bm

5 Em	Bm	G	A⁷

Example 3

TRACK 1 / 13

♩ = 84 **Country**

Gm	Dm	Cm	F

5 Cm	Gm	E♭	D⁷

Example 4

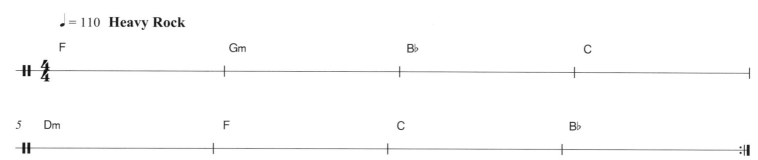

> **TOP TIP** Some of the improvising examples at this grade feature swung quavers (eighth notes), which you should be able to hear on the backing track. Listen carefully to the track to help you capture the feel of swung quavers in your performance.

Example 5

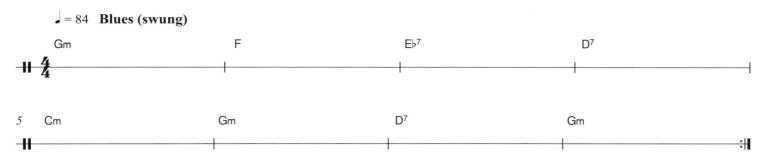

Example 6

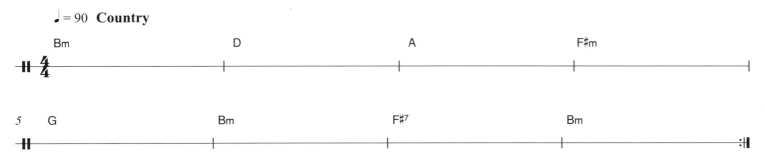

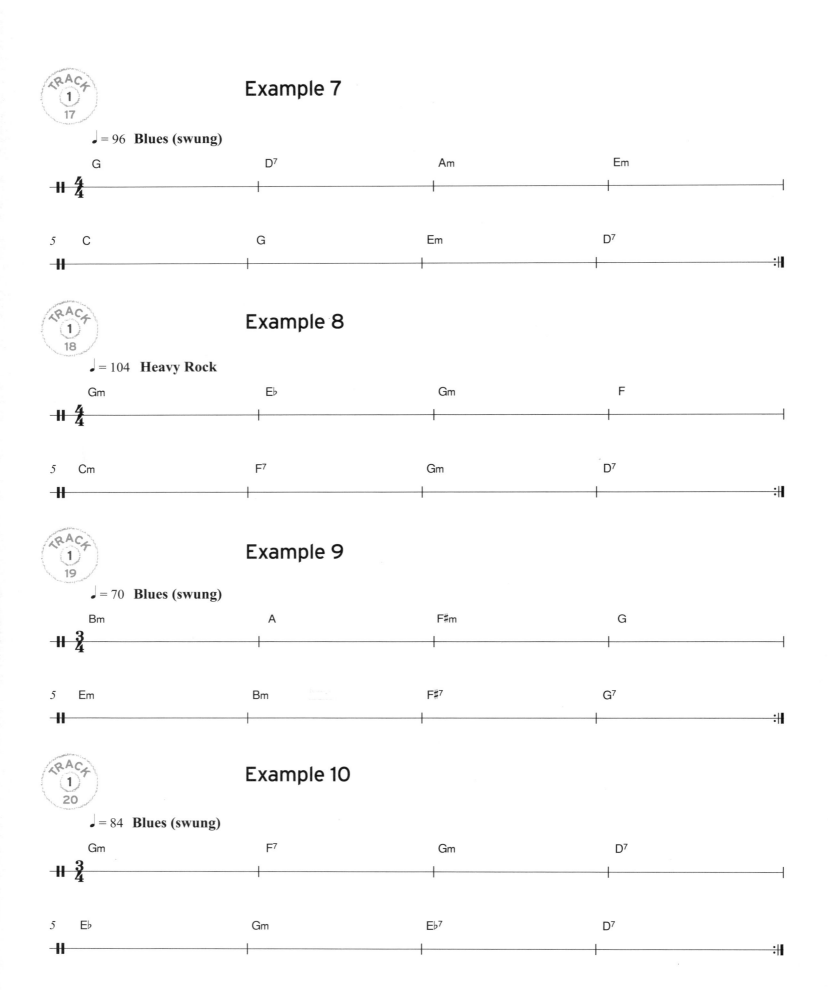

Example 7

TRACK 1 · 17

♩ = 96 **Blues (swung)**

| G | D⁷ | Am | Em |

5 | C | G | Em | D⁷ |

Example 8

TRACK 1 · 18

♩ = 104 **Heavy Rock**

| Gm | E♭ | Gm | F |

5 | Cm | F⁷ | Gm | D⁷ |

Example 9

TRACK 1 · 19

♩ = 70 **Blues (swung)**

3/4 | Bm | A | F♯m | G |

5 | Em | Bm | F♯⁷ | G⁷ |

Example 10

TRACK 1 · 20

♩ = 84 **Blues (swung)**

3/4 | Gm | F⁷ | Gm | D⁷ |

5 | E♭ | Gm | E♭⁷ | D⁷ |

GRADE 4 PLAYBACK

Example 1

 **TOP TIP** Look out for the $\frac{6}{8}$ time signature which is featured in playback from Grade 4 onwards. This will flow best if you try to feel two beats per bar with three quavers (eighth notes) in each beat.

Example 2

Example 3

Example 4

Example 5

Example 6

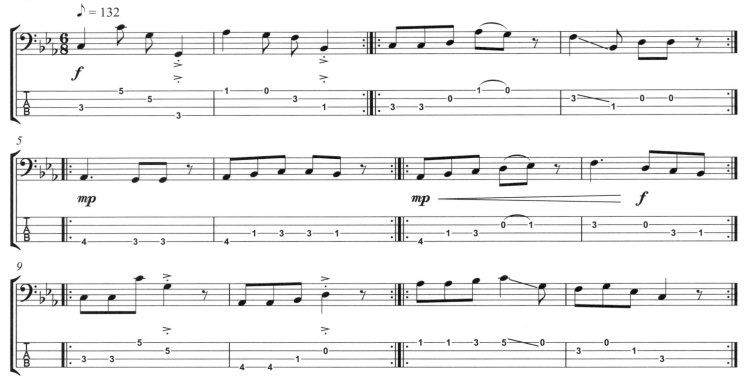

Example 7

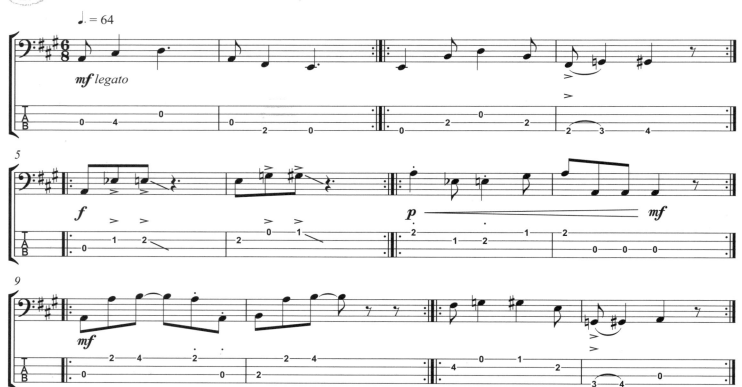

Example 8

Example 9

Example 10

 Notice the *crescendos* and *diminuendos* which are featured in playback at this level. These are most effective if you perform them evenly, getting gradually louder or quieter over the full duration of the *crescendo* or *diminuendo*.

GRADE 4 IMPROVISING

Example 1

$\quad$ = 65 **Reggae**

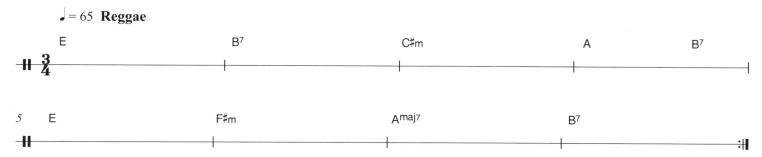

Example 2

$\quad$ = 58 **R 'n' B**

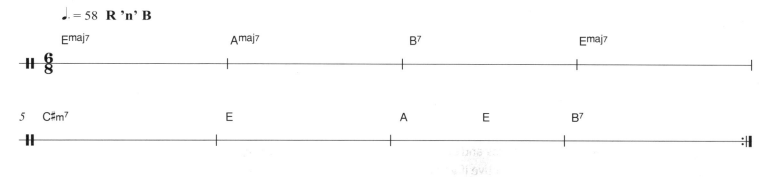

TOP TIP Reggae and R'n'B are new styles for improvising at this grade. Listen to plenty of music in these styles to get the feel for them.

Example 3

TRACK 1 33

♩ = 84 **Reggae**

Cm	E♭	Fm⁷	B♭⁷

4/4

5 G⁷	A♭maj7	Fm⁷	Dm⁷ G⁷

Example 4

TRACK 1 34

♩ = 80 **Country**

E	Amaj7 B	F#m⁷	C#m

4/4

5 B⁷ E	Amaj7	F#m⁷ E	A

Example 5

TRACK 1 35

♩ = 76 **R 'n' B**

Cm	B♭	E♭	A♭ B♭

3/4

5 Cm	Fm⁷	Gm⁷	G⁷

Example 6

TRACK 1 36

♩ = 72 **Reggae**

Cm⁷	Gm⁷	A♭maj7	B♭⁷ G⁷

4/4

5 Cm⁷	Fm⁷	A♭maj7 G⁷	Cm

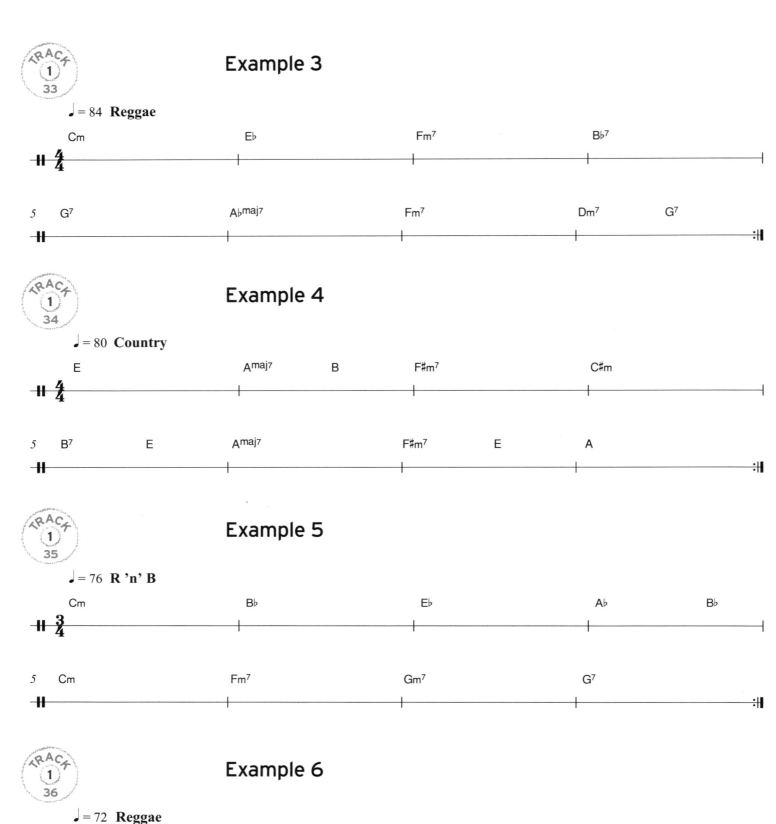

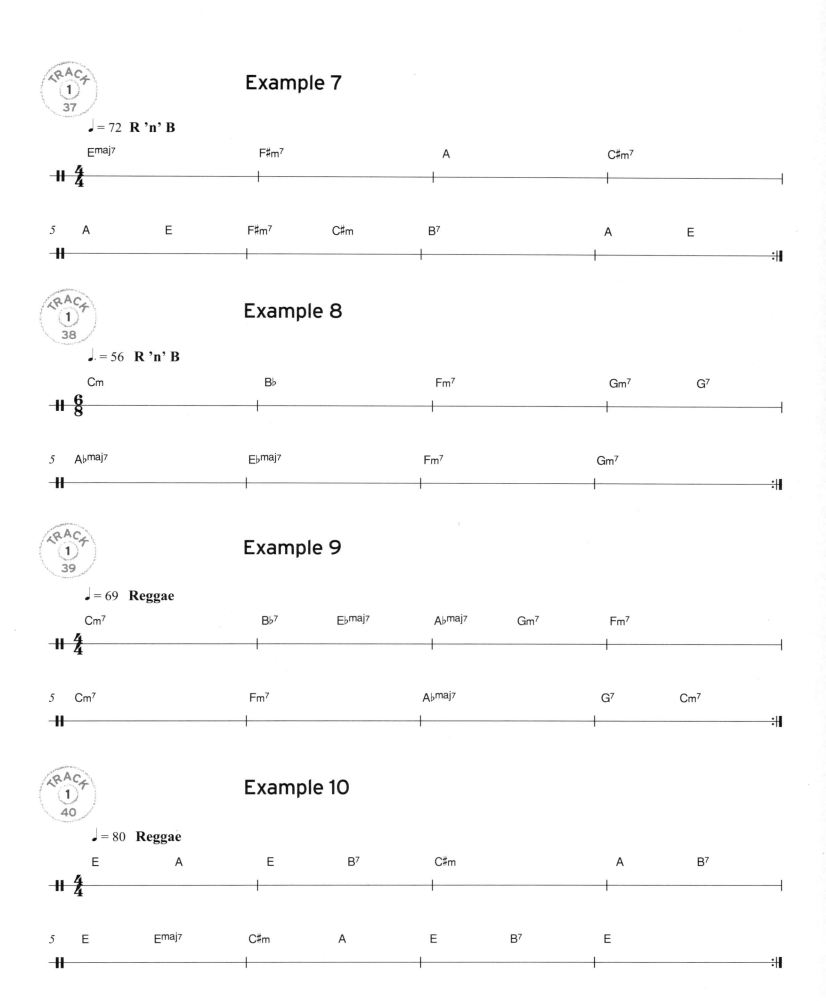

GRADE 5 PLAYBACK

TRACK
2
1

Example 1

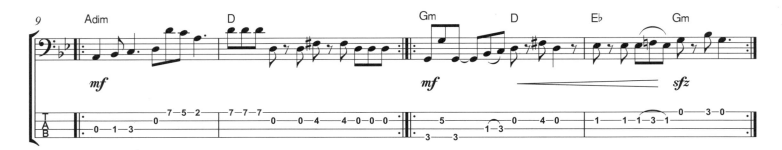

Example 2

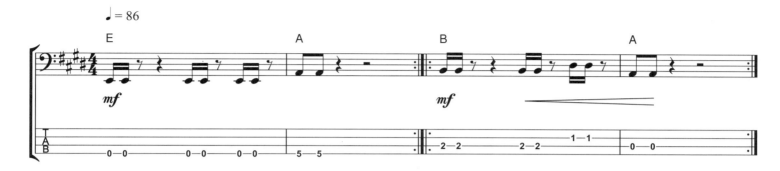

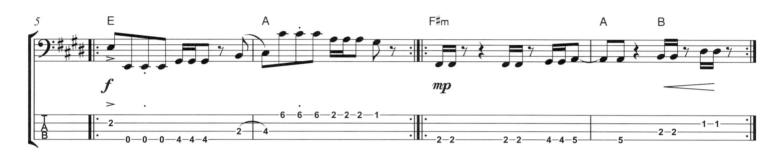

 **TOP TIP**   Notice the slide in the last bar of this example. It is one of several small musical details in this example, along with accents and *staccato*. Do your best to capture these details to achieve an effective performance at this level.

Example 3

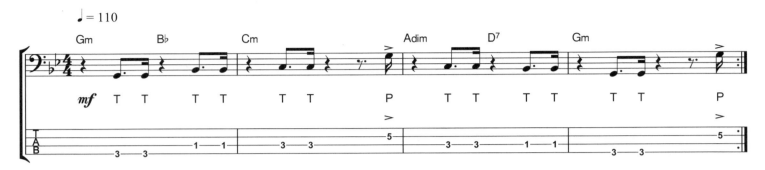

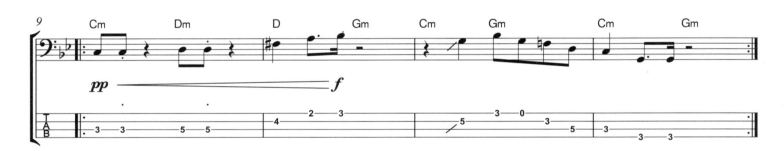

Example 4

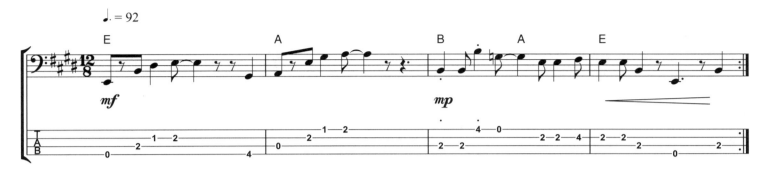

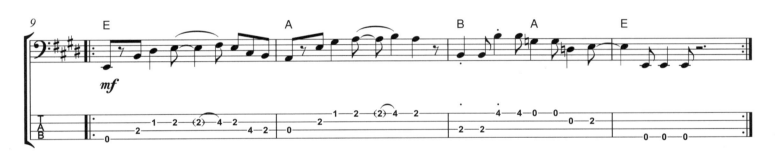

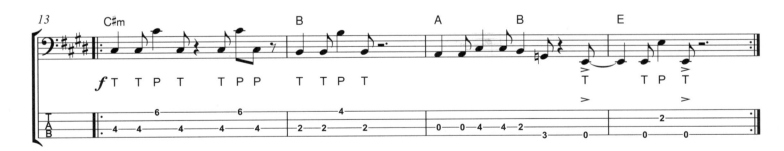

Example 5

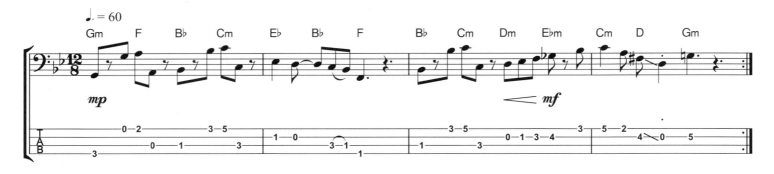

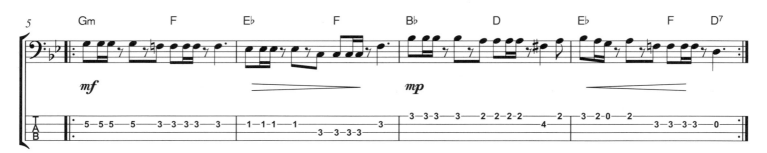

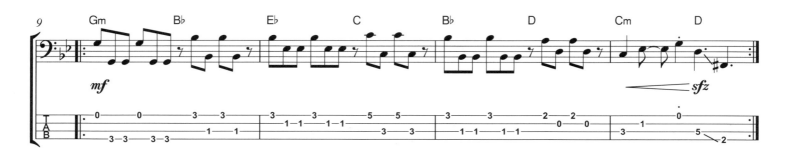

Example 6

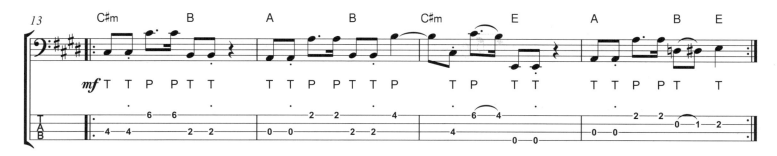

Example 7

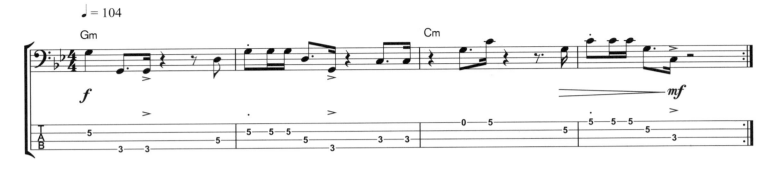

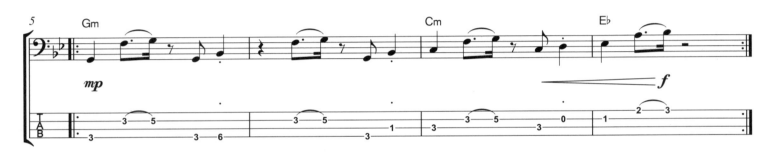

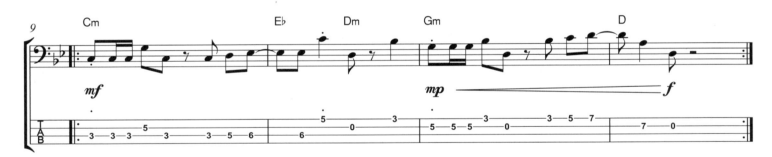

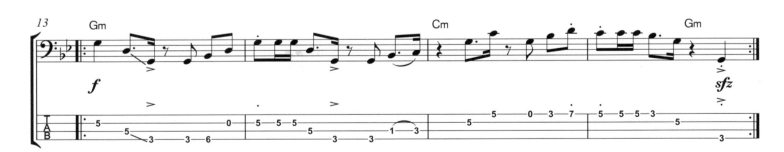

Example 8

Example 9

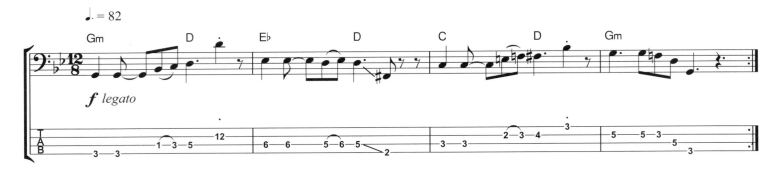

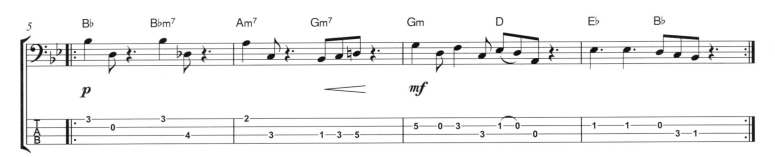

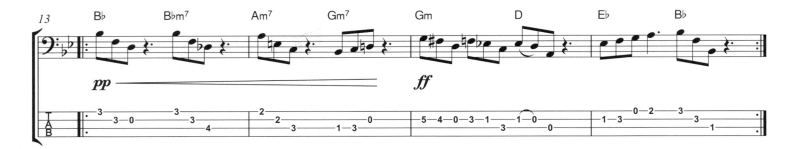

Example 10

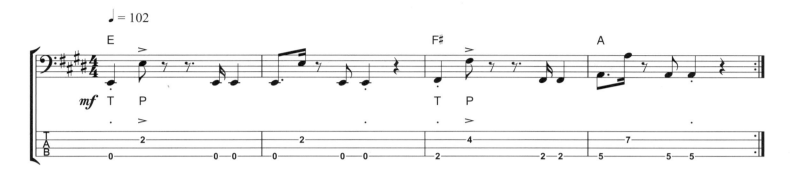

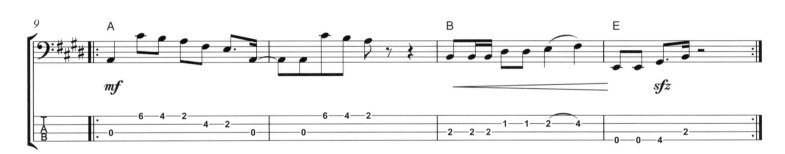

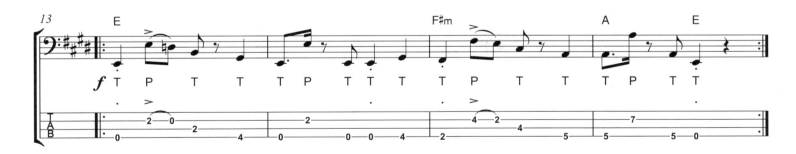

GRADE 5 IMPROVISING

Example 1

♩ = 102 **Funk**

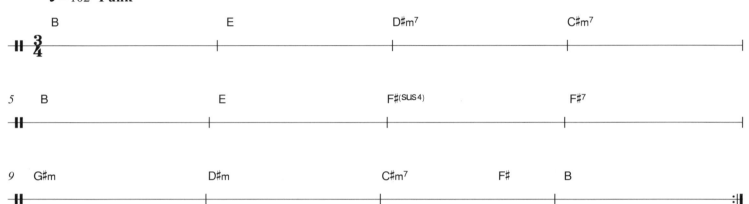

| B | E | D#m⁷ | C#m⁷ |

| B | E | F#(SUS 4) | F#⁷ |

| G#m | D#m | C#m⁷ | F# | B |

Example 2

♩. = 63 **Shuffle**

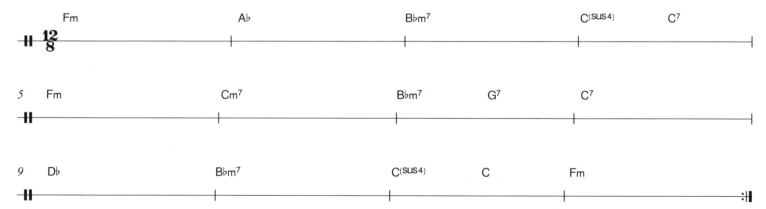

| Fm | A♭ | B♭m⁷ | C(SUS 4) | C⁷ |

| Fm | Cm⁷ | B♭m⁷ | G⁷ | C⁷ |

| D♭ | B♭m⁷ | C(SUS 4) | C | Fm |

Example 3

♩ = 104 **Disco**

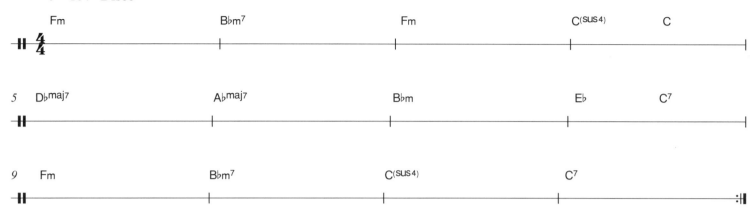

Fm	B♭m⁷	Fm	C⁽ˢᵘˢ⁴⁾ C
5 Db^maj7	A♭^maj7	B♭m	E♭ C⁷
9 Fm	B♭m⁷	C⁽ˢᵘˢ⁴⁾	C⁷

Example 4

♩ = 100 **Shuffle**

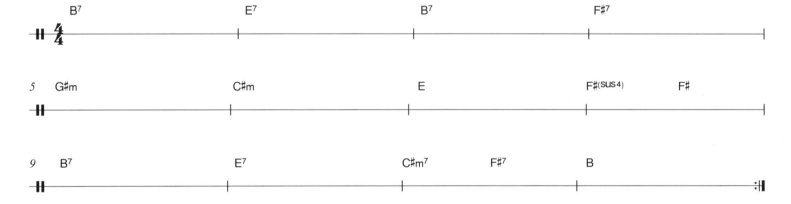

B⁷	E⁷	B⁷	F♯⁷
5 G♯m	C♯m	E	F♯⁽ˢᵘˢ⁴⁾ F♯
9 B⁷	E⁷	C♯m⁷ F♯⁷	B

TOP TIP Notice that there are sometimes two different chords in each bar at this level. Listen for these changes in the backing track and try to find notes that sound good with each chord.

Example 5

TRACK 2 15

♩ = 100 **Disco**

| G | C | G | D⁷ | Em | | Am⁷ | D⁷ |

4/4

| 5 Bm⁷ | Em⁷ | Am⁷ | D(sus4) | D⁷ |

| 9 G | C | D⁷ | Em | Am⁷ | D⁷ | G |

Example 6

TRACK 2 16

♩. = 88 **Funk**

| B | G♯m⁷ | F♯⁷ | C♯m⁷ | E | F♯⁷ |

12/8

| 5 G♯m | D♯m | C♯m⁷ | F♯(sus4) | F♯⁷ |

| 9 B | G♯m⁷ | F♯⁷ | E | F♯⁷ | Bmaj7 |

Example 7

TRACK 2 17

♩. = 76 **Funk**

| Fm⁷ | E♭ | Fm⁷ | B♭m | Cm⁷ | Fm |

12/8

| 5 D♭ | B♭m⁷ | Fm⁷ | A♭maj7 | C(sus4) | C |

| 9 Fm⁷ | E♭ | Fm⁷ | B♭m | Cm⁷ |

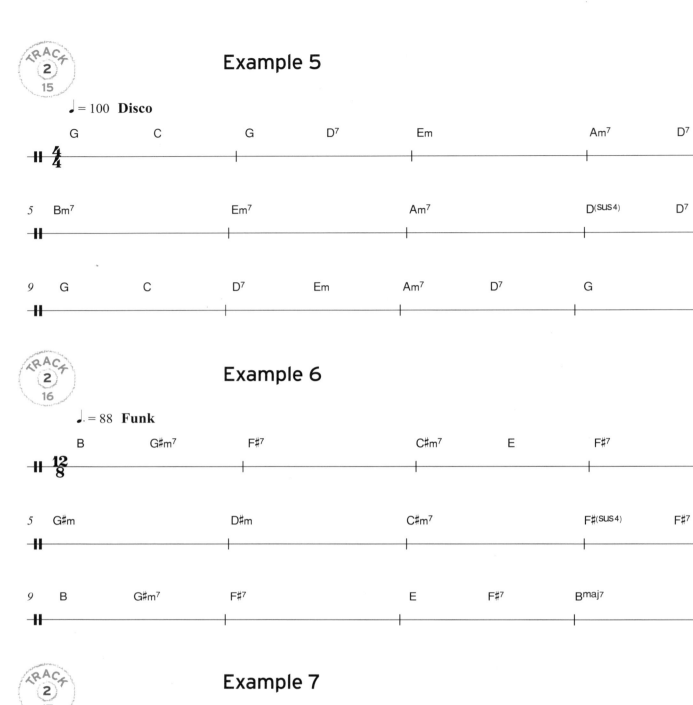
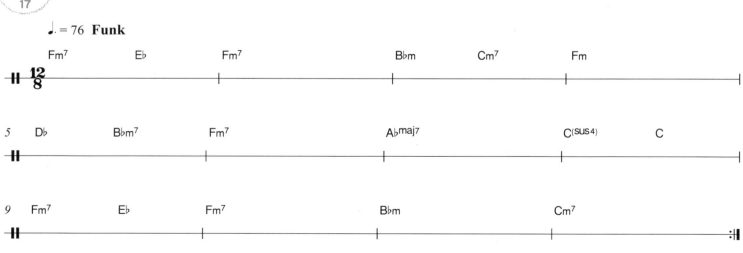

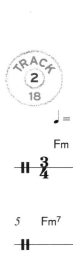

Example 8

♩ = 92 **Shuffle**

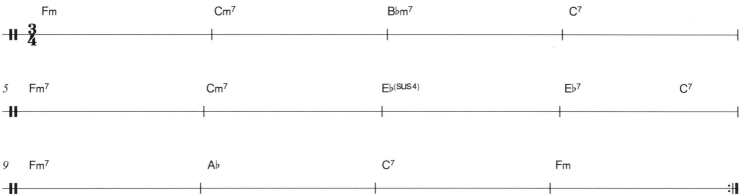

| Fm | Cm⁷ | B♭m⁷ | C⁷ |

| 5 Fm⁷ | Cm⁷ | E♭(sus4) | E♭⁷ | C⁷ |

| 9 Fm⁷ | A♭ | C⁷ | Fm |

Example 9

♩ = 110 **Disco**

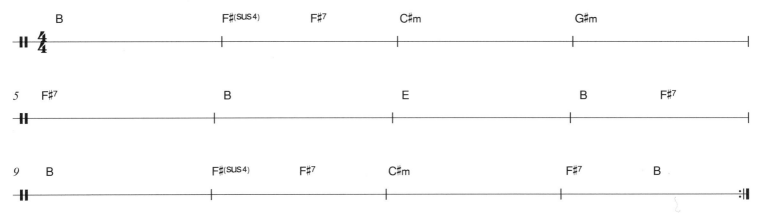

| B | F♯(sus4) F♯⁷ | C♯m | G♯m |

| 5 F♯⁷ | B | E | B F♯⁷ |

| 9 B | F♯(sus4) F♯⁷ | C♯m | F♯⁷ B |

Example 10

♩. = 92 **Funk**

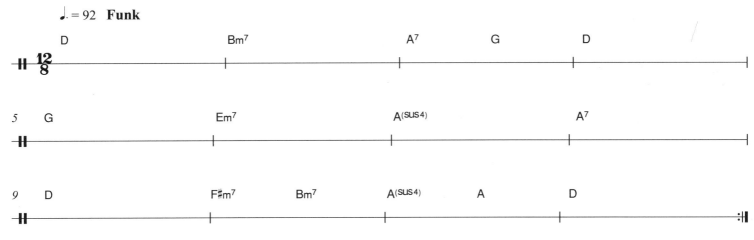

| D | Bm⁷ | A⁷ G | D |

| 5 G | Em⁷ | A(sus4) | A⁷ |

| 9 D | F♯m⁷ Bm⁷ | A(sus4) A | D |